THE CAPTAIN LAI

THE CAPTAIN
LANDS IN
PARADISE

POEMS BY

SARAH MANGUSO

Alice James Books
FARMINGTON, MAINE

Grateful acknowledgment is made to the following publications in which these poems first appeared, sometimes in slightly different forms:

American Letters and Commentary: "The Rider," "Social Theory"; *The American Poetry Review*: "The Deer Comes Down the Mountain," "It's a Fine Thing To Walk Through the Allegory"; *The Best American Poetry 2001*: "The Rider"; *Boston Review*: "Wild Goose Chase"; *Chicago Review*: "The Precision We Need Is of Another Earth"; *Conduit*: "Poem of Comfort"; *The Iowa Review*: "The Dunes in Truro," "Two Variations on a Theme by Stevens," "What I Found"; *Jubilat*: "Address to Winnie in Paris"; *Lit*: "Give Me a Sign"; *The New Republic*: "Poem of Comfort in Which I Am Powerless"; *Poetry Daily*: "Two Variations on a Theme by Stevens"; *The Spoon River Poetry Review*: "Short Essay on the Muse," "Another Poem About the Muse."

Epigraph text from *The Log of Christopher Columbus* (tr. Robert H. Fuson, International Marine Publishing Co., a division of Highmark Publishing, Ltd., Camden, Maine, 1987) reproduced with permission of The McGraw-Hill Companies.

Cover image from "Portolan World Map" by Andreas Homen (1559), published in *The Cartography of North America: 1500–1800* (Pierluigi Portinaro and Franco Knirsch, White Star Edizione, Vercelli, Italy, 1987).

Numberless and sincere thanks to my parents, teachers, and friends.

Alice James Books gratefully acknowledges support from the University of Maine at Farmington and the National Endowment for the Arts.

13 12 11 10 9 8 7 6 5 4

Alice James Books are published by the Alice James Poetry Cooperative, Inc., an affiliate of the University of Maine at Farmington.

ALICE JAMES BOOKS
238 MAIN STREET
FARMINGTON, MAINE 04938

www.alicejamesbooks.org

LIBRARY OF CONGRESS CATALOGING-IN-PUBLICATION DATA
Manguso, Sarah, 1974–
    The captain lands in paradise: poems / by Sarah Manguso.
        p. cm.
ISBN 978-1-882295-33-3
I. Title.
PS3613.A353 C37 2002
811'.6—dc21   2001038422

CONTENTS

I

The Rider   3

The Deer Comes Down the Mountain   4

It's a Fine Thing To Walk Through the Allegory   5

The Truth   6

The Piano   7

Prospect   8

I Was Waiting Patiently   9

Beautiful Things   10

American Reverie   11

Social Theory   12

Poem of Comfort   13

Poem of Comfort in Which All Things Are the Same   14

Poem of Comfort in Which I Am Powerless   15

Wild Goose Chase   16

II

Address to Winnie in Paris   19

The Precision We Need Is of Another Earth   21

What I Found   23

The Bartender in Hell   24

Telling Lies   25

Clytie and Her Sun 26

The Captain Lands in Paradise 27

The Questioners 28

Love Is a Narrative Impulse 29

Short Essay on Love 31

Glencoe 32

Putting the Cat Together 33

Narrative Poem 34

Short Essay on the Muse 35

There Is a Difference Between 36

The Typewriter 37

III

Another Poem About the Muse 41

The First Time 42

Two Variations on a Theme by Stevens 43

Space 44

What We Miss 45

Winter Poem 46

The Dunes in Truro 47

Cha-Cha 48

The Snow 49

The Chair 50

The Inkstain 51

The Barn 52

The Hurricane 53

Love Story With Bad Moral 54

Give Me a Sign 55

I have seen all the East and West, and I have traveled through Guinea, but in all those regions harbors as perfect as these will never be found. And it has been the case that each harbor I have come to has been better than the last one. I have considered what I have written very carefully, and I assert I have written correctly and that now this harbor surpasses all the others. All the ships of the world could be contained in it, and it is so sheltered that the oldest line on the ship would hold it fast.

—*Christopher Columbus, February 21, 1493.*

I

The Rider

Some believe the end will come
in the form of a mathematical equation.
Others believe it will descend as a shining horse.
I calculate the probabilities to be even at fifty percent:
Either a thing will happen or it won't.
I open a window,
I unmake the bed,
Somehow, I am moving closer to the equation
or to the horse with everything I do.
Death comes in the form of a horse
covered in shining equations.
There will be no further clues, I see.
I begin to read my horse.
The equations are drawn in the shapes of horses:
horses covered in equations.
I am tempted to hook an ankle
around the world as I ride away.
For I am about to ride far beyond
the low prairie of beginnings and endings.

The Deer Comes Down the Mountain

Now we gather worshipful.
The gears in his legs shine down.
He lifts his head.
Here he comes!
We're erecting a maypole with green ribbons.
His legs are four probes.
And his back is a ship
And his eyes are holes in the curtain.
We're eating cookies in the shape of him.
The icing is gold and silver.
He's shedding gears, here he comes tripping!
He is casting off the elastic bindings.
Now we're hanging giant flags.
The wind-up key sticks in his side like a blade.
The wind rocks him on his wheels.
Here he comes, crawling!
The bright obvious shines in his body.
Here comes the electric, the burning mystery!

It's a Fine Thing To Walk Through the Allegory

It's a fine thing to walk through the allegory
and emerge in a cruise ship with a heap
of artificial flowers and a cake
with oranges. What is this all about? Sometimes
the real meaning moves from the specific
to the general, as in the famous essay
about symbols and allegories where, in the end,
everything's about God—earth, air, water,
fire, dancing on the upper deck in a green dress.
The big secret is what's growing down there,
roundish, dark, about the size of an orange.
You have no idea it's there. You have no idea
what it means—it's either an orange or cancer.
The real meaning moves from the specific to the general
but writing even a hundred poems about the same deer
is not necessarily about God. Would a deer
eat an orange if it were properly salted?
It would be like God eating an orange, or a deer
wearing a green dress and taking a bite out of God.
It's a fine thing to walk through the orange grove
and emerge in the middle of nowhere with an armload
of something salty and ominous—either a giant cake
tainted by the sea air or the cancerous carcass
of a deer preserved in a box with artificial flowers—
but at least this time you're holding everything
you can see until the last still moment.

The Truth

This is as much as we knew:
The truth was an infinite list.
The truth was a box of nouns.
I fell into the truth, trying to explain it.
I wrote in two hands—one was better.
The census taker came to count me.
His name, God help him, was Frank.
The truth shone out of the dirt on his shoes.
It was better than me.
It destroyed my stuff.
It blinded me; it was so dark; it was so bright.
What happened next was indeed true:
All the people lined up in rings around the earth.
The truth came in the form of a powerful verb.
It happened in time.
It happened to everything in the box.
It formed the border between itself and itself.
An invisible bar horizoned in both directions,
the people lifting it or swinging.
It moved so quickly it became a sphere.
On one side of it was the truth.
On the other side was the truth.
I woke up from dreaming of myself dreaming of myself.

The Piano

I try to imagine the lid closing but it won't.
The keys shine at me in black and white.
They are evil. I am evil. My dream is evil.
I whisper the word *concupiscence* into the open lid,
Which is a sin. I am so full I cannot breathe.
The stars arc overhead. I am in a field.
The piano has followed me here—softly, softly.
It spits music at me, then blankets me in music.
I put it on a leash as an experiment.
It whimpers, then is still. No music comes.
I fall in love with my pet.
We walk through the field.
The piano spells my name in keys.
It plays me a piece I have never heard
Rolling gently behind me—it begins
with the sound of light moving
and ends with the sound of a sun going out.
They are the same even though the picture changes.
I make love to my piano in the open field.
I have nothing to do with the universe.
I prefer to stay here with you.

Prospect

When the closed piñata falls from its tether
we play slow-pitch with a fuel log.
Gone is the green frog!
No more beautiful dreams!
Strangers come with their six-fingered hands
and scoop up the booty, burrowing
for the splinters even, wise to be small
as they are. And I leave the park with nothing
in my pocket but a slip of paper bearing a few lines
of scrawled braille, my best ideas written across my throat
in blue letters. Back home I nail a disco ball
to the northwest corner of the floor.
The light rearranges itself. I whisper to the holes
in the wall from which the small animals come in their sleep
walking over craters of sweet imaginary food.
When the street lights go out I cover the ball
and forget where it is. I steer the animals back
into the wall to save them from embarrassment,
taking care not to name any of them, coughing slightly
from an allergy, preparing to memorize the anatomy
of the animals my animals will give birth to tonight
after the light fades and I do not notice the light—
my enemies have stolen my eyes and left them rolling
in the park's dark center. Now they are weeping slightly.
Now the field is full of light.
Now they are winking, aphids gathering in the canthi,
taking turns yielding to the wind, shedding their four corneal layers
one by one, a tarantella for the vitreous humor
that leaves them now in silver threads. They are barely
anything at all to look at, soap bubbles lying in dust.
They look at the tree, look up, look at the sun.
Each looks at the other.

I Was Waiting Patiently

It was cold. I stayed under my hat.
I knew that soon it would be time for my destiny.
I thought I was something in the way of prepared, as one is
the night of the induction trying on three different hats,
one after the other, and while doing so
dropping the index cards under the desk.
It was my whole destiny that was coming,
birds alighting on me while I stood in the north forty
the way they did on St. Francis, although I am no saint
with my silver arms outstretched,
holding up my pages to the eternal ceiling.
And I am no country boy. And surely I am no chess player,
waiting for the final check. But soon I might become
exactly what I am not, as a pupa wakes up
to become what appears an entirely different species.
I am simply myself, lying around,
maybe shining or burning in this time, practicing
for the next without meaning to. I may sob true love now,
but just around the corner a truer love awaits.
I may sip drinks through a straw and roll under the table,
burbling drunk, but what's coming next is the truest sin,
the shiniest car, the softest bed,
the swingingest partner at the sock hop
dancing and enchanted under the sea, and my own true destiny.

Beautiful Things

Sometimes I think I understand the way things work
and then I find out that on Neptune it rains diamonds.
On this world you can get out of work early, unclog the drain,
hear music. Any of the above should prove the existence
of God or at least some kind of beautifying engine
but in Germany when they couldn't figure out
how to tranquilize the polar bear and he was standing
in the park, the cage door broken, they shot him dead.
Nine hundred pounds—that's a lot of dead bear.
Neptune's pretty close to immortal,
as we understand the word, and I wouldn't like to be
that planet. But if I had to I would take it,
the decades of punishing rain, and the fires
on neighboring planets I would watch,
thankful I was never touched by them,
and that the diamonds were mine.

American Reverie

Every verb form is happening simultaneously
and it is no picnic, especially
when the seagulls circle in a swarm
and refuse to pick up the garbage,
choosing instead to punish us
with their incessant hunger.
I forgot what was hidden
out on the guarded promontory
but I see a family and you see a family
and out on the windy spit are all my families,
stretching back into the centuries with no trains,
when a paved road meant with stones,
and dinner meant cooked game,
and someday there I'll be, supine, staring
unblinking up at the earth, somewhere
when there is one small, maybe catered, event
and then the giant idea of it.
I forget which is which and which is worse,
and *one nation under God* is just the beginning
of the list of things I never understood, right
before *land of the pilgrims' pride* or was it *plight*,
and the lifeguards wade out halfway to the breakers
in their blue uniforms—how can they know
what it is to save me, drowning in a lake
moving like boiling soup because the earth
spins and shakes and refuses to die, refuses
to fly heavenward and meet its cold moon?

Social Theory

It was time for a social theory.
People were just standing around.
The penalty for creating new languages was death:
for oneself, one's family, and nine related families.
I was putting drinks on tables
and walking away from them.
The piano lying on its side
represented the degree of my unhappiness.
I was only trying to find my drink
and to communicate without lying—
all the while the people sang
to the dust on the piano and I was writing
the last sentences in the world that were true.
If I didn't become anything,
at least I would have that much.
A dark stranger, maybe my social theory,
stood around with its hands in its jacket pockets.
It was drinking from all my glasses.
I couldn't stop it.

Poem of Comfort

An anonymous freezer-box full of violets
drops down but it's unimportant, love.
Remember the missile trails all converging
but the city was still there
after the gas station and we never knew
what the hell they were,
and all those nightmares of frozen blue pyramids
chunking down to crush baby animals,
true,
and what about birds who die mid-flight?
certainly no stranger or rarer than having
an aneurysm on the trading floor.
Gravity here means justice, or at least some kind of God,
for whom or what there are limits. I don't believe any of it
but what comfort is there in that?
So, love, look away from the dying marsupials,
for I am about to invent a distracting brand-new dance
to deliver you from all the thundering disparity of the world.

Poem of Comfort in Which All Things Are the Same

Let's go to Greece
where every island is a different color
and look at the ruins that predict their own shapes,
and the dogs that bark in them.
Now you are naming each building
and I'm carrying you inside a building,
your judgments following behind us like a history.
Keats lies in some different ruins,
those more of baths than of sofas,
and pieces of his hair decay above ground in fancy libraries.
Chances are you will not see a single ghost in your lifetime
but many objects that might be mistaken for ghosts.
Every country in the world has invented ghosts,
and how they find us. This poem is new.
This poem is for you.

Poem of Comfort in Which I Am Powerless

I hold an empty tub
to the sky above your head
to arrest any ill-behaved stars
while you are a non-swimmer
in a boatful of dangerous crewmates.

Extravagant city!
where I run ahead and tape over some lights
on every block leaving you a beautiful spectrum
and half bent over behind you an alcoholic witch
takes a few things out of your pockets.

In winter with all the windows shut
I stare up into the white corners with my net
and if the bats come catch them
and if the goats come catch them
and if the ants come catch them.

Wild Goose Chase

My desperation was like that—
I was clambering up a fire escape on Houston Street
in hot pursuit while there it was,
lying on a beach in Oregon.
If I could only perceive it, see how large it was,
and be persuaded of its finitude.
You share a detail and I share a detail
and there we are, boring one another
with such sad banalities as we deserve.
I thought I recalled my adversary
playing chemin-de-fer on B Deck
but it was only me, sitting in a red dress,
imbibing red drinks. I can't
always recognize myself. Who's there?
or there? Pluck the tune on a zither,
carve the words on a stone slab. Make something,
anything. My desperation called to me, murmuring,
I leaned in to kiss it, and it was gone.
The source of it, deep in some distant volcano,
had to be quenched. I was all set
to go on an important journey, to buy
the phrasebook and read it on the boat, getting ready
for the cool wind across my face, fires burning in the sky
and the geese of mourning crossing overhead
as if in a daze and as if themselves an indication of hope.

II

Address to Winnie in Paris

Winnie, I am writing this on behalf of my friend Harris. He loves you and wants you to love him. I have never been to Paris, but I have heard that it is a good place to be in love in.

The Arc de Triomphe is real. The Jardin des Tuileries is real. The Eiffel Tower is very real. The carafe of wine, the remains of dinner, the bill: all real. None are necessary to your life.

Harris has confided that he enjoys dating. To profess such a thing is to advertise a facility for one kind of loneliness, which has nothing to do with the other kind: the one you did not know was there until afterward.

The part of the betrayal which wounds the most is hearing that it has already happened.

Diderot writes that the word is not the thing, but a flash in whose light we perceive the thing. Plato wrote of the need to be reconjoined with the rest of oneself. My analyst speaks of codependent impulses in modern society. These various explanations are metaphors for an inaccessible truth.

In de Laclos, a betrayal is an invitation to a string of further betrayals, each one taking you further from the original. If the hell for lovers consists in being betrayed, the hell for the beloved consists in betraying. These hells comprise the world.

A much older friend writes: Most romances do not last, and it is best to forget them. Tolstoy writes: All happy families are alike. My teacher says: Bad poems are all bad for the same reason: imprecision.

Around you move many seas. It is impossible not to drown a little. In Bulfinch's, an anchor is let down into the garden. This is to remind us that we live underwater.

Up above the high-water mark, angels with their teeth and their sharp little wings watch us with murderous disinterest. They sentence us for the one crime we all commit.

It is said by area doctors that cowboys notoriously misrepresent their degree of pain. For this reason their diseases progress far beyond the point at which treatment is beneficial. Are they lying?

If I could read only one sentence for the rest of my life, it would be the one where the jailer says to Socrates *I can see that you are a good man, the best one that has ever been in this place.*

These examples are meant to dissuade you, Winnie, from loving men other than my friend Harris. He asked me to write this poem.

Arvol Looking Horse, a Sioux leader, called Devils Tower *the heart of everything that is.* Very large objects remind us of the possibility of the infinite, which has no size at all. But we understand it as something very, very large.

What the lover seeks is the possibility of return, the strange heart beating under every stone.

The Precision We Need Is of Another Earth

It is claimed by certain Indian yogis that suspended animation is indeed possible, that the heart may be stopped and maintain silence underground for a period of hours or days.

But you just can't fake the breakdown of the cell wall, the mysterious foam, the opaque eye.

Can't fake the "child" emerging from behind the "curtain."

According to Buber, the Zulu word for *far away* is *there where someone cries out, O mother, I am lost.*

Some people argue that, in order to know anything at all, you have to do drugs all day long.

So come O clarity and bear me away on your silver arms! Come out and teach me stuff!

On one hand, this is an appeal to the universe. On another, it is a love letter to a sailor, the first sailor in the world—that is, the one who guides his craft beyond the empyreal doorjamb.

On the other side, a voice: *Hello, sailor!*

As I age, things become clearer—clearer and clearer. Saying that is a sort of joke.

Withered are the leaves, naked is the sky above my head. Where has the time gone? Was I not just a child?

Childhood consists of misunderstanding things you have no right including in your childhood.

Gass writes: Life is not a sign and therefore has no meaning.

But there are certainly "signs of life," as when the smacked-out moll twitches a thumb, starts to emerge from her coma. The signs mean that someone is alive.

So what does it mean when the men parachute from the rocky tip and float down the glen like a snowstorm of angels?

On parachuting from the tops of mountains: The worst that can happen is you find yourself on top of a barn—with two broken legs.

The stairs between the second and third floors tilt rakishly to the left and down. I worry about the third floor falling down onto the second.

As for the second floor floating up to meet the third, I worry I won't be there when it happens.

What I Found

I finally found what makes things light and carried away a large pail of it.

On the way back I met a fat man and offered to paint some on his feet. He said it gave a lovely floating sensation in his shoes mostly.

I still had a lot left so I dipped some animals in it. They spun at about waist height like spitted carcasses.

After that things got out of hand. Schoolchildren carried it in their pockets and caused the chalk to levitate. Everything was in the air. People were tired of it and wanted me to get rid of the rest of it so I mixed it with sand and threw it in the sea. Since then it has not stopped raining...

The Bartender in Hell

I was a bartender in hell.
People were coming up to the bar and asking for drinks
And I was saying *there aren't any drinks here.*
This is hell. I didn't have any drinks.
I didn't even have any glasses.
But I had to stay there.
A figure approached, sat down on a burning stool.
I know you don't have any drinks, he said. *It's all right.*
He went on. *I was a painter while on earth.*
I could do some painting here to fill the hours.
I have some canvases that the flames never touch
But they themselves burn whitely.
I am surrounded by thousands of canvases, he said.
But the only color I have is white,
Staring back at me, wicked and eternal…

Telling Lies

I enjoy lying.
I don't know how to tell a story, but I hide this fact
so artfully they don't notice I'm lying.
Here I sit, waiting for the phone to ring.
Lies! Are you coming to get me?
Are you coming with an armload of blankets?
My two favorite parameters inform the things I say
and the way I say them. More lies every day!
Ninety-nine blocks away lives my other life,
waking up now and wiping his nose on the blanket.
Now he's doing his exercises and getting in the car.
He can't find the lies! Driving around,
doing errands, he stops at a mailbox,
drops in hundreds of letters, all lies.
Now he emerges from the market, carrying bags.
There is no way to ascertain this.
Now he's charging up a hill, chasing a snow leopard,
catching it by the paws, wrestling it to the ground.
It spits. One of its eyes slowly closes.
A lie! It snaps awake and eats its captor, groceries and all.
I'm taking notes. When I return to the office after lunch
I'll write it longhand. I'll make the leopard a bighorn sheep
and the wrestler another sheep leaning against it.
I'll make the groceries a bundle of twigs and leaves.
I'll make the blanket a little forest.
They won't believe a word of it.

Clytie and Her Sun

after Ovid

Now I am standing still.
My head moves as you drive the day across.
You blackened my face. You made my dress whiter.

The waving of the stem following.

I am showing you my white dress.
I am holding up the hem.
Now I am stretching my face, reaching.
I can see the clouds burning. I think you are watching me.

The face wider, black as the girl's pupil in daylight.
The halo gold in reflection.
What the sun would see if it looked down for a moment…

The Captain Lands in Paradise

Many bodies determine the course, wheeling, your small instrument extending what the eye sees. The difference between the air's sweep and the sea's rising equals your movement, even over the land as your two legs move you no closer to the twin seas that contain you. The course, you write, is the opposite of stillness measured. Moving through things that move lies your end, and the wind stirs them further, and the moving takes you there—you are moved and the air is what moves you and your ship is stopped by nothing stopping.

An edge of land sealed in the glass. *This is for time. Our path is wide, simple, and new. We cut through it as this land falls. As long as we are here it will not stop falling...*

The Questioners

We have read too many books.

Just before the key modulates,
a tone sounds more like its position in the old key
than it sounds like its position in the new key.

That is, it sounds more like the present than the future,
but the future is imminent in it,
as in a sculpture life is imminent.

I raise my hand in the studio
but no one of authority looks at me.

Only the other questioners look at me,
their hands raised and limply waving.

We are all equally ashamed, making a soft noise together,
in the studio gently waving.

We are lowering our hands now, all equally ashamed.

Love Is a Narrative Impulse

In the beginning I am tottering around Boston
in the mid '70s, pasting things together.
In the beginning self-knowledge is not crucial.
E. steals my heartmobile,
M. cries when someone takes away his pretty leaf.
Construction paper is everywhere
and when it is replaced by panic I do not notice.
When it is suggested I write a dictionary,
I come up with one entry:
Bike—something you ride.
I don't remember wanting a bike
as brutally as I remember wanting gum.
Warhol swore he survived solely on candy and cake.
The relative worth of objects is clear to me.
I have to write a report on glass.
I like the way calendars hurricane open in old movies.
I develop a crippling stage fright
between the audition and the first rehearsal.
Jean Cocteau, asked what he would save
if his house were on fire, replied *the fire*.
Because everything said in assembly is true
I save a feather from a great horned owl for 18 years.
When the pizza sign gets fixed I miss the flicker.
I really have practiced dancing with a broom.
I think I can measure everything.
Here I am, armed with a sextant
and a handful of plastic rulers. The first time
I see my friend smoke we are sitting in a field.
Asleep in the tepee I miss out
on my final night of vigilance.
No one in our whole photography class
does the assignment called Sky Meets Ground.
The best building in New York City

is the downtown municipal building with the angel.
When I laugh my grandmother says
You have the same face flying through.
Luminiferous ether—there was no such thing!
I listen to the first live recording of "Yesterday"
and wonder what made the girls scream there,
and there, and there.

Short Essay on Love

I was in the alley and then I was in the restaurant.
Something had happened and I didn't know what it was.
All I knew was I was changed.
The train goes into the tunnel and comes out the other side;
the trembling child emerges from behind the curtain.
Unchain my heart, thou monstrous god.

This is a picture of love: two gondolas in the dark.
This is also a picture of love: a hill covered with snow
and in the distance just within view...a snowman.

Once I learned how to read the lines on the side of my hand,
I was never the same.
A love story: I am cold and happy
and then sleep on the divan and wake up sad.
In the morning I use the dusty toothbrush
that doesn't belong to anyone. Love?
Practice riding on a skateboard in an empty street at night.

Go to a high school football game.
Everybody there knows what love is.
Another love story:
I think there is a knife in my head somewhere.
Another: There was only one picture of me, and I took it.
Remember the names of towns.
Give birth to something that looks like you.

Glencoe

The sheep cling to the side of Ben Nevis,
permanent as tears. I disembark from the ski lift,
the sheep laughing as I walk out of the valley
and into the parking lot. When do you stop walking
and start driving? The sun stays out all summer,
arctic winds blowing through the heath.
The piper stands wide as a house, weights hidden
in the bottom of his kilt. I've come to come clean, lugging
my woe in plastic bags. I'm going to water the ground.
Innocent as eggs, the sheep look at me looking at them.
Each one blinks as if trying to remember my face.

Putting the Cat Together

She ordered fifteen sacks of bones for us,
and some red clay—to simulate the blood
the things had lost, their flesh stacked in the cans.
We spent whole afternoons playing with bits
of red and bone. Each group had half a cat
to put together. Some devised a jaw
that shut and opened as a living one
would shut and open. Some just picked among
the bits that held a shoulder muscle taut
along the bone—pieces that looked like dust
to me. We were eleven. And the thought
that poignancy commands the things we do
did not occur to us, for we lived in
the world. And it would be a long time yet
before we knew the way that, grieving for
us, the mystery would announce itself.

Narrative Poem

At a party in January an entire shelf of books
fell on some teenagers.

They weren't expecting it.
They found it delightful and newsworthy.

The boy thought he had lost the girl,
and then she came out into the poetry.

He was prepared for a formal goodbye
when he began choking on fruit.

Ashamed of the narrative of his life,
he ignored the cat lying on the floor
where the other cat had lain.

But the ignorant steps he took spelled something,
visible from space, slowly on the world.

And when they saw the satellite had fallen
into the atmosphere and burned,
the physicists cried.

And the story failed to become the story.

Short Essay On the Muse

The engineer catches an accidental in the seventh movement, flipping switches at it, waving tuning forks. Hearing one note sung can inspire the carefullest lie. I saw the same girl twice on the same corner—we were walking in opposite directions but the second time in reverse. *She must come now*, no one thinks, not me, not knowing which girl, and there she is. Hearing one note sung, hearing it bright and unthought before you expect it, comes before the wish. Usually it's sounds or shapes in the grass. Yes, those are deer on the lawn, and the wish comes true before you make it. If only there were a doe! First, something pale and unnameable, and then the scurry to invent her.

There Is a Difference Between

A room in which others obstruct the view and one in which every-thing is concealed by sheets. You might even be grateful, although there would be some throat-clearing. You might just miss the hindquarters of something tucking itself in. Or a tree with pink—something. When a corner of the cloth lifts, you look away, just in case. If you wanted to, you could remember anything.

The Typewriter

Little knives in the machine insist on recording everything not once, but twice—or, as you suspect, three times, but you will never know for sure until some careful soul cuts you open and employs the scientific method. The paper, the ribbon, the head. *Ticka-ticka-ticka-tick.* Somewhere, all grown up, is the boy from home who once said you were beautiful but strange. You have since stopped trying to be one and not the other. Somewhere along the way you may have made a terrible mistake. Are the knives in the back of the drawer pointing in the wrong direction? It will be days before you notice. If you met him again you might never think to ask. Somewhere on the earth there is a drawerful of knives pointing the other way. Somewhere there is a list, and you have chosen the wrong thing.

III

Another Poem About the Muse

Now the deer are far away and it's raining. The muse drives by in a sil-
ver pickup, wheels digging furrows. The deer neither approach nor
flee, but stand against a background of pure mathematics, both
approaching and fleeing. From a distance a deer can resemble a
machine of stainless steel. And the eyes might be open or not. There is
Thursday, but then there is Friday. There is a grief, or a loss, repre-
sented by a deer. With the right artificial preparations, a mechanical
deer could leave behind a steaming footprint. The furrow of it sinks.
And the shape of you coming in close is not the same as the shape of
you leaving.

The First Time

The first time I saw sunlight strike the earth in columns I was amazed it had been possible all along. I wrote down the date and time as proof so it would stay true. And I thought I couldn't peel away after the kiss and ever be the same, but as it turned out there was no sudden rescrambling on the molecular level. *O let me not be changed!* I would exclaim. There are many ways of knowing, as anyone who has studied epistemology can tell you. Watching a beautiful back is enough to do it. M. says he'll call at ten and calls five minutes before. Love? All that remains is to write the beautiful fiction.

Two Variations on a Theme by Stevens

First there is the thing and then there is
the account of the thing, bent into new
alphabets. Living your life twice is no feat.
Or there is what happens to you, as if
to you only, the yes of no comparison,
until finally, or secretly, the yes
repeats. So a vine with grapes enough
to persuade it to the ground may be a line
with one grape repeated. All love's sighs
are this, simply: an inhalation, an
exhalation, something in between that
is imagined. The final word is the first word
reiterated with gray hair.

Much like mine, your delight.
No discrete evidence of the new
is invented. For the other suns are
our sun surrounded similarly, not seen
together. Some uncertain planet is
what one wants it to be, until found,
when it is the earth. The documents
of genius are nightmares with the sentences
rearranged. Your aspirations
to magnificence are already done
and recorded as the memoirs of sad kings.

Space

Moon unfolds like a fan, snaps in, winks out.
In this time you say you haven't moved,
but a certain wet little planet has spun and spun.
When the plane dips, you hold the arms of the seat.
You say it would make sense to hold
something outside, arms at least,
or a double cumulus handful,
or something higher,
and you wonder about the higher things.
For names abound,
names you don't have things for.
Recall that the universe
expands slightly more each day,
how each time it rains
the drops are traveling further.
We live in a space
where telescopes impale a moving body
that is stationary in its own way,
as is, for instance, Neptune,
coldest of any planet save Pluto,
whose rings are theoretical
and therefore imaginary,
but nevertheless may spin more quickly
than the body they surround, dressed in winds
and made still by them
and prepared by them
for the faraway naming of seas.

What We Miss

Who says it's so easy to save a life? In the middle of an interview for the job you might get you see the cat from the window of the seventeenth floor just as he's crossing the street against traffic, just as you're answering a question about your worst character flaw and lying that you are too careful. What if you keep seeing the cat at every moment you are unable to save him? Failure is more like this than like duels and marathons. Everything can be saved, and bad timing prevents it. Every minute, you are answering the question and looking out the window of the church to see your one great love blinded by the glare, crossing the street, alone.

Winter Poem

Either great dignity or the lack of it prevents people from tearing down buildings they no longer need.

When the deer run through the cabin, the air moves aside to accommodate them. The walls expand and contract, admitting and expelling deer.

It is a physics problem.

To the unschooled, everything under the layer of smooth muscle looks like a heart, including cancer, even though it's mostly water.

Upon waking, one of the first things to do is to replace the water exhaled in the night. Sometimes it shows on the windows.

Throw out the middle step and you're breathing ice.

Winter has everything to do with the heart and lungs.

When the boy throws the girl in the snowdrift, the shape she leaves in the snow looks nothing like her.

When the snow melts around the cavity, will you recognize her?

The Dunes in Truro

A girl walks up the dunes with the aid of a cane, trying not to get sand in her heart. All around her, very beautifully, houses fall in the ocean and disappear. At least one thing is being prevented. The creeping mountains reconstitute. They are moving in some direction. It is like surfing, but very slowly. William Harvey discovered the circulatory system in 1616. *It must therefore be concluded,* he wrote, *that the blood in the animal body moves around in a circle continuously, and that the action or function of the heart is to accomplish this by pumping. This is the only reason for the motion and beat of the heart.*

Cha-Cha

We are moving like an iceberg across the floor.
We have some chairs
stolen from the dining room downstairs.

Sometimes I forget to bend my knees,
and then I am a soft windmill.

It is difficult to keep from laughing
the laugh that has come three times in my life:
Once in a kickball game
when I touched the ball and made it fly.
Once listening to a girl sing Bach
too beautifully in a church in East Germany.

I am laughing now remembering
when I never was a dancer in a black dress,
spinning and sliding on green tiles.

The Snow

Someone else shared his first sentence. *The snow falls here in white sheets.* We were leaving for a new place, but it was one we had read about. *The snow falls here quietly and muffles. The snow falls here when you aren't looking.* Then on the plane I imagined drawing in the snow there, living in it, raising a family in it. The snow would be deep enough to sculpt. People would get lost in it. The snow, my snow, would fall not only in sheets, but in pillars and ropes and cascades. There would be cities made entirely of snow. Then we took turns describing the ice-people we would find hiding in their watery castles. When the plane landed, we found barely a dusting, as though drawn on—as though it could be wiped clean away with one hand.

The Chair

The night the crier stacked a knife box on two chairs, and we took it all, was the same night the birds came. We stood the chair on the porch and went out for some bourbon, and across the street the trees had filled with crows. It was unaccountable. A clutch of kids staggering home saw them too and called out *hoo, hoo,* and the crows flew somewhere—each to a different pole? I went back and sat in the chair. It had a smell about it, old smoke, but it would do. The room had needed a chair. It was late. On the other side of the door the cat was crying out all the pain of its life.

The Inkstain

A boy who didn't love me back gave away a shirt with an inkstain from eighteen years earlier. I wore the shirt and the stain faded and disappeared by the end of summer—it was a miracle. I kept wearing the shirt and eventually forgot its significance, and on every birthday I grew less worried that I might forget to grow older. Like everything you remember, the anticipation of growing is lost steadily but incompletely. It goes slowly, and when the great miracles come you fail to recognize them.

The Barn

There was a barn in the middle of two camps—boys on one side, girls on the other. I never crossed over, but it was said that the boys lived in tepees. There was a path that grew less distinct and then suddenly was under trees. I do not remember ever bathing the whole first year. The inside of the barn was all of the same wood. Were the walls carved with initials, each one important? They must have been. So many people must have been kissed there. It was something old, so much older than me, so much older than I would ever get to be. The last dance was later, after I had stopped remembering. I danced one time with someone who asked me, and as soon as I draped my arms over his shoulders I stopped remembering. What I do remember is the first resistance of his clavicles under my wrists and the knowledge that the ceiling of the barn was above me somewhere, far away and dark. That about the ground there was a yellow light, as if there were a fire burning somewhere. It was the longest I had ever touched someone.

The Hurricane

An entire afternoon looking up, maybe throwing a ball. The shape of
the sky through the trees. The trees, and the shape of that sky, and the
woods' shape below. It was not quite the country, and I knew this,
lying on the picnic table in winter—everything white and almost
silent—supine, trying to feel something. The spring we had the hurri-
cane I was old enough to take note of certain facts. My mother was sit-
ting in our yellow-lit cellar listening to a portable radio. The voices on
the radio sounded wrong because of the way she had set the tuner. I
knew afterward my father had been outside, had seen the stretched-out
power lines. Our neighbor was also there. Since then I have made it a
picture—old lady standing in the wind, arms out, dogs behind her—
dogs pressed against a wall, she about to fly, three blind dogs hooting,
she flying, they buoyant on the air, riding and not knowing why, not
knowing that what they saw of the storm was all I saw.

Love Story With Bad Moral

I already felt like an empty sink sitting there in my slip. And I could have skipped breakfast altogether and not noticed. Nevertheless this is not a logical argument against breakfast. There are always plenty of people who would if—something. I don't know why I'm here. I often return to the scene of the crime. Oh I have loved and lost, and oh there is no explanation. When I asked my mother what she was thinking when she got married she said she was thinking, *Well, I'll be able to get out of this, too.* When two people see each other again they will pick up where they left off. In the paper a man from New Guinea speaks in the aftermath of a tidal wave. *The people will go back, but to a better place*, he says. *We will build new homes away from the sea.*

Give Me a Sign

The moon rises in the planetarium and something seems about to—if only you knew where to look. You keep blinking but not one body looks familiar. Like the boy in the film you believe in one thing, guard it jealously. But you are different from the boy. The boy dreamt of the sea, a French sea. When he found it he thought *so this is the sea.* Perhaps if you stare long enough the stars spell something, but you are distracted by the uncomfortable bench. It is important to follow the rules—if you make enough of them, you might get somewhere. The boy in the film has nothing to do with you—after all, he was French. You have never even been to France, and you would go if you could only decide whether all the beautiful girls in Montmartre would make you unhappy. It's still dark. Nothing is happening. The moon is still pasted on the ceiling and there are no clouds. It is so clear—it's as clear, as they say, as day.

RECENT TITLES FROM *Alice James Books*

Ladder Music, Ellen Doré Watson
Self and Simulacra, Liz Waldner
Live Feed, Tom Thompson
The Chime, Cort Day
Utopic, Claudia Keelan
Pity the Bathtub Its Forced Embrace of the Human Form,
　　Matthea Harvey
Isthmus, Alice Jones
The Arrival of the Future, B.H. Fairchild
The Kingdom of the Subjunctive, Suzanne Wise
Camera Lyrica, Amy Newman
How I Got Lost So Close to Home, Amy Dryansky
Zero Gravity, Eric Gamalinda
Fire & Flower, Laura Kasischke
The Groundnote, Janet Kaplan
An Ark of Sorts, Celia Gilbert
The Way Out, Lisa Sewell
The Art of the Lathe, B.H. Fairchild
Generation, Sharon Kraus
Journey Fruit, Kinereth Gensler
We Live in Bodies, Ellen Doré Watson
Middle Kingdom, Adrienne Su
Heavy Grace, Robert Cording
Proofreading the Histories, Nora Mitchell
We Have Gone to the Beach, Cynthia Huntington
The Wanderer King, Theodore Deppe
Girl Hurt, E.J. Miller Laino
The Moon Reflected Fire, Doug Anderson
Vox Angelica, Timothy Liu
Call and Response, Forrest Hamer
Ghost Letters, Richard McCann
Upside Down in the Dark, Carol Potter

ALICE JAMES BOOKS has been publishing exclusively poetry since 1973. One of the few presses in the country that is run collectively, the cooperative selects manuscripts for publication through both regional and national annual competitions. New authors become active members of the cooperative, participating in the editorial decisions of the press. The press, which places an emphasis on publishing women poets, was named for Alice James, sister of William and Henry, whose gift for writing was ignored and whose fine journal did not appear in print until after her death.

TYPESET AND DESIGNED BY MIKE BURTON

Printed in the USA
CPSIA information can be obtained
at www.ICGtesting.com
JSHW080007150824
68134JS00021B/2329